# Some *of* GOD'S Miracles

Some *of* GOD'S Miracles
Copyright © 2022 by Vincent A. Piccone, M.D.

Published in the United States of America

| ISBN | Paperback: | 978-1-959761-04-4 |
| ISBN | eBook: | 978-1-959761-05-1 |

All rights reserved. No part of this publication may be reproduced, stored in a retrieval system or transmitted in any way by any means, electronic, mechanical, photocopy, recording or otherwise without the prior permission of the author except as provided by USA copyright law.

The opinions expressed by the author are not necessarily those of ReadersMagnet, LLC.

ReadersMagnet, LLC
10620 Treena Street, Suite 230 | San Diego, California, 92131 USA
1.619. 354. 2643 | www.readersmagnet.com

Book design copyright © 2022 by ReadersMagnet, LLC. All rights reserved.

Cover design by Kent Gabutin
Interior design by Daniel Lopez

# Some *of* GOD'S Miracles

Vincent A. Piccone, M.D.

ReadersMagnet, LLC

# INTRODUCTION

This book is about miracles of God that are cited in the Bible. The first miracle in the Bible is the creation sequence itself where God creates the universe and everything that is in it. The Bible is filled with incredible happenings and events that were outside human experience. These include healings, acts contrary to the natural order, and supernatural events. Many of the miracles in the Bible were performed by Jesus in the New testament though there was evidence of these events in the old testament. In the old testament miracles pointed to the work of God in the world. In the new testament the miracles of Jesus point to the fact that he was the Son of God.

*Some of God's Miracles*

The miracles of God are present in the world today as God continues to show men his glory, power, and majesty. Miracles happen in almost everyone's life and can be recited if we are careful to note them. Whether it be a fatally sick person that gets better or an intervention in a persons life that causes a dramatic personality change miracles are all around us.

The author has taken examples in the Bible of miracles completed by God to illustrate the divine power. Examples of miracles include the plagues of Egypt, the raising on the dead, the restoration of hearing and sight in the deaf and blind, the cure of lepers, the cure of various diseases to include dropsy, leprosy, paralysis, and all the other diseases. Physical miracles include the manna, the feeding of thousands with little, the production of the widow's oil, walking on water, the calming of storms, turning the water into wine, and the production of droughts and floods.

Aside from the miracles that Jesus granted his apostles and disciples to perform, only God can perform miracles. God, the divine physician, alone can restore the withered hand and stop the hemorrhage in a woman who no physician could cure. He alone can make the sun stop. Jesus alone can by his word, raise the dead and cure the woman of fever. Based on the fact that miracles are unexplainable the author will only describe the miracles and not give the science behind them. In fact there is no science behind them.

Faith is a key element to miracles, they are often performed in people who believe the miracle can be performed. Without faith there is often absence of a miracle. As when Moses was punished by striking the rock twice to perform the miracle of water gushing from the rock to provide the Israelites with water so we may be punished by our lack of faith in God to perform miracles.

Miracles were often performed by the word and touch of Jesus. Healings were especially completed by the touch of Jesus and sometimes by his word.

The author has not included all the miracles in the bible. Joshua asking God for help in battle results in the sun stopping for a full day so the Israelites can win a war. Similarly there is the miracle of sunlight traveling in an opposite direction as a sign that a man will get better. There is the fleece that becomes wet and dry in response to a request so that one may know the will of God. There is the Snakebite of Saul in the books of acts that does not kill him despite the fact that the viper bite should have killed him. Elijah prays to God for a drought and God responds with three and one-half years of no rain. The fall of Jericho and the collapse of the walls of the city happens miraculously. Then there is the contest between the prophets and false prophets wherein a holocaust offering is consumed despite being doused with water. There are the miracles in Jesus life- His birth to a virgin.; the transfiguration ; the institution of the Eucharist; the resurrection of Jesus, and the ascension of Jesus.

# MUCH OUT OF LITTLE

A man came from Baal-shalishah bringing the man of God twenty Barley loaves made from the first fruits, and fresh grain in the ear, Elisha said, "Give it to the people to eat." But his servant objected, "How can I set this before a hundred?" Elisha again said, "Give it to the people to eat, for thus says the LORD: You will eat and have some left over." He set it before them. And when they had eaten, they had some left over, according to the word of the LORD. 2 Kings 4:42-44

A certain woman, the widow of one of the guild prophets, cried out to Elisha : "My husband your servant is dead. You know that he revered the LORD, yet now his creditor has come to take my two children into servitude." Elisha answered her, "What am I to do with you? Tell me what you have in the house." She replied, "This servant of yours has nothing in the house but a jug of oil." He said, "Go out borrow vessels from all your neighbors—as many empty vessels as you can. Then come back and close the door on yourself and your children; pour the oil into all the vessels, and as each is filled, set it aside." So she went out. She closed the door on herself and her children and, as they handed her the vessels, she would pour in oil. When all the vessels were filled, she said to her son, "Bring me another vessel." He answered, "There is none left." And then the oil stopped. She went and told the man of God, who said, "Go sell the oil to pay off your creditor; with what remains you and your children can live." 2 Kings 4:1-7

When Jesus heard of it, he withdrew in a boat to a deserted place by himself. The crowds heard of this and followed him on foot from their towns. When he disembarked and saw the vast crowd, his heart was moved with pity for them and he cured their sick. When it was evening. The disciples approached him and said, "This is a deserted place and it is already late; dismiss the crowds so that they can go to the villages and buy food for themselves." [Jesus] said to them, "There is no need for them to go away; give them some food yourselves."

But they said to him, "Five loaves and two fish are all we have here." Then he said, "Bring them here to me," and he ordered the crowds to sit down on the grass. Taking the five loaves and the two fish, and looking up to heaven, he said the blessing, broke the loaves, and gave them to the disciples, who in turn gave them to the crowds. They all ate and were satisfied, and they picked up the fragments left over—twelve wicker baskets full. Those who ate were about five thousand men, not counting women and children. Matthew 14:13-21

Jesus summoned his disciples and said, "My heart is moved with pity for the crowd, for they have been with me now for three days and have nothing to eat. I do not want to send them away hungry, for they may collapse on the way." The disciples said to him, "Where could we ever get enough bread in this departed place to satisfy such a crowd?" Jesus said to them, "How many loaves do you have?" "Seven," they replied, "and a few fish." He ordered the crowd to sit down on the ground. Then he took the seven loaves and the fish, gave thanks, broke the loaves, and gave them to the disciples, who in turn gave them to the crowds. They all ate and were satisfied. They picked up the fragments left over—seven baskets full. Those who ate were four thousand men, not counting the women and children. And when he had dismissed the crowds, he got into the boat and came to the district of Magadan. Matthew 15:32-39

When he disembarked and saw the vast crown, his heart was moved with pity for them, for they were like sheep without a shepherd; and he began to teach them many things. By now it was already late and his disciples approached him and said, "This is a deserted place and it is already very late. Dismiss them so that they can go to the surrounding farms and villages and buy themselves something to eat." He said to them in reply, "Give them some food yourselves." But they said to him," Are we to but two hundred days' wages worth of food and give it to them to eat?" He asked them, "How many loaves do you have? Go and see." And when they had found out they said, "Five loaves and two fish." So he gave orders to have them sit down in groups on the green grass. The people took their places in rows by hundreds and by fifties. Then, taking the five loaves and the two fish and looking up to heaven, he said the blessing, broke the loaves, and gave them to [his] disciples to set before the people; he also divided the two fish among them all. They all ate and were satisfied. And they picked up twelve wicker baskets full of fragments and what was left of the fish. Those who ate[ of the loaves] were five thousand men. Mark 6:34-44

In those days when there again was a great crowd without anything to eat, he summoned the disciples and said, "My heart is moved with pity for the crowd, because they have been with me now for three days and have nothing to eat. If I send them away hungry to their homes, they will collapse on the way, and some of them have come a great distance." His disciples answered him, "Where can anyone get enough bread to satisfy them in this deserted place?" Still he asked them, "How many loaves do you have?" "Seven they replied. He ordered the crowd to sit down on the ground. Then, taking the seven loaves he gave thanks, broke them, and gave them to his disciples to distribute, and they distributed them to the crowd. They also had a few fish. He said the blessing over them and ordered them distributed also. They ate and were satisfied. They picked up the fragments left over— seven baskets. There were about four thousand people.

He dismissed them and got into the boat with his disciples and came to the region of Dalmanutha. Mark 8:1-10

*Some of God's Miracles*

When the apostles returned, they explained to him what they had done. He took them and withdrew in private to a town called Bethsaida. The crowds, meanwhile, learned of this and followed him. He received them and spoke to them about the kingdom of God, and he healed those who needed to be cured. As the day was drawing to a close, the twelve approached him and said dismiss the crowd so that they can go to the surrounding villages and farms and find lodging and provisions; for we are in a deserted place here." He said to them, "Give them some food yourselves." They replied, "Five loaves and two fish are all we have, unless we ourselves go and buy food for all these people." Now the men there numbered about five thousand. Then he said to his disciples, "Have them sit down in groups of [about] fifty." They did so and made them all sit down. Then taking the five loaves and the two fish, and looking up to heaven, he said the blessing over them, and gave them to the disciples to set before the crowd. They all ate and were satisfied. And when the leftover fragments were picked up, they filled twelve wicker baskets. Luke 9:10-17

After this, Jesus went across the Sea of Galilee [of Tiberius] A large crowd followed him, because they saw the signs he was performing on the sick. Jesus went up on the mountain, and there he sat down with his disciples. The Jewish feast of Passover was near. When Jesus raised his eyes and saw that A large crowd was coming to him, he said to Philip, "Where can we but enough food for them to eat?" He said this to test him, because he himself knew what he was going to do. Philip answered him, "Two hundred days' wages worth of food would not be enough for each of them to have a little [bit]. One of his disciples, Andrew, the brother of Simon Peter, said to him, "There is a boy here who has five barley loaves and two fish; but what good are these for so many?" Jesus said "Have the people recline." Now there was a great deal of grass in that place. So the men reclined, about five thousand in number. Then Jesus took the loaves, gave thanks, and distributed them to those who were reclining, and also as much of the fish as they wanted. When they had had their fill, he said to his disciples, "Gather the fragments left over, so that nothing will be wasted." So they collected them, and filled twelve wicker baskets with fragments from the five barley loaves that had been more than they could eat. When the people saw the sign he had done, they said, "This is truly the prophet, the one who is to come into the world. "Since Jesus knew that they were going to come and carry him off to make him king, he withdrew again to the mountain alone. John 6:1-15

The above miracles manifest that God can produce much out of little. God fed the Israelites manna out of thin air for forty years as they traversed the Sinai peninsula. From the old testament God feeds many from twenty barley loaves. The widow receives much oil at the instruction of the prophet, In the new testament God feeds thousands on multiple occasions through the blessing of Jesus with much left over. It is impossible by physical law to explain how the loaves and fish were multiplied. Bread and fish were produced out of thin air.

## OUT OF THE MOUTHS OF LIONS

Darius decided to appoint over his entire kingdom one hundred and twenty satraps. These were accountable to three ministers, one of whom was Daniel; the satraps reported to them, so the king should suffer no loss. Daniel outshone all the ministers and satraps because an extraordinary spirit was in him, and the king considered setting him over the entire kingdom. Then the ministers and satraps tried to find grounds for accusation against Daniel regarding the kingdom. But they could not accuse him of any corruption. Because he was trustworthy, no fault or corruption could be found in him. Then these men said to themselves, "We shall find no grounds for accusation against the Daniel accept in connection with the law of his God." So these ministers and satraps stormed in to the king and said to him, "King Darius, live forever! All the ministers of the kingdom, the prefects, satraps, counselors, and governors agree that the following prohibition ought to be put in force by royal decree: for thirty days, whoever makes a petition to anyone, divine or human, except to you O king, shall be thrown into a den of lions. Now, O king, let the prohibition be issued over your signature, immutable and irrevocable according to the law of the Medes and Persians." So king Darius signed the prohibition into law.

Even after Daniel heard that this law had ben signed, he continued his custom of going home to knell in prayer and give thanks to his God in the upper chamber three times a day, with the windows open toward Jerusalem. So these men stormed in and found Daniel praying and pleading before his God. Then they went to remind the king about the prohibition: "Did you not sign a decree, O king, that for thirty days, who ever makes a petition to anyone, divine or human, except to you, O king, shall be cast into a den of lions?" The king answered them, "The decree is absolute, irrevocable under the law of the Medes and Persians." To this they replied, "Daniel, one of the Jewish exiles, has paid no attention to you, O king, or to the prohibition you signed; three times a day he offers his prayer." The king was deeply grieved at this news and he made up his mind to save Daniel; he worked till sunset to rescue him. But these men pressed the king. "Keep in mind, O king," they said, "that under the law of the Medes and Persians every royal prohibition or decree is irrevocable." So the king ordered Daniel to be cast into the lions' den. To Daniel he said, "Your God, whom you serve so constantly, must save you." To forestall any tampering, the king sealed with his own ring and the rings of the lords the stone that had been brought to block the opening of the den.

Then the king returned to his palace for the night; he refused to eat and he dismissed the entertainers. Since sleep was impossible for him, the king rose very early the next morning and hastened to the lions' den. As he drew near, he cried out to Daniel sorrowfully. "Daniel, servant of the living God, has your God whom you serve so constantly been able to save you from the lions?" Daniel answered the king: "O king, live forever! My God sent his angel and closed the lions' mouths so that they have not hurt me. For I have been found innocent before him; neither have I done you any harm, O king!" This gave the king great joy. At his order Daniel was brought up from the den; he was found to be unharmed because he trusted in his God. Then the king ordered the men who had accused Daniel, along with their children and their wives, to be cast into the lions' den. Before they reached the bottom of the den, the lions overpowered them and crushed all their bones.

Then King Darius wrote to the nations and peoples of every language, wherever they dwell on the earth: "May your peace abound! I decree that throughout my royal domain the God of Daniel is to be reverenced and feared: "For he is the living God, enduring forever, whose kingdom shall not be destroyed, whose dominion shall be without end, A savior and deliverer, working signs and wonders in heaven and on earth, who saved Daniel from the lions' power." So Daniel fared well during the reign of Darius and the reign of Cyrus the Persian. Daniel 6:2-29

When the Babylonians heard this, they were angry and turned against the king. "The king has become a Jew," they said; "he has destroyed Bel, killed the dragon, and put the priests to death." They went to the king and demanded: "Hand over Daniel to us, or we will kill you and your family." When the king saw himself threatened with violence, the king was forced to hand Daniel over to them. They threw Daniel into a lions' den, where he remained six days. In the den were seven lions. Two carcasses and two sheep had been given to them daily, but now they were given nothing, so that they would devour Daniel.

The prophet Habakkuk was in Judea. He mixed some bread in a bowl with the stew he had boiled, and was going to bring it to the reapers in the field, when an angel of the Lord told him, "Take the meal you have to Daniel in the lions' den at Babylon." But Habakkuk answered, "Sir, I have never seen Babylon, and I do not know the den!" The angel of the Lord seized him by the crown of his head and carried him by the hair; with the speed of the wind, he set his down in Babylon above the den. "Daniel, Daniel," cried Habukkuk, "take the meal God has sent you." You have remembered me, O God," said Daniel; "you have not forsaken those who love you." So Daniel tae, but the angel of God at once brought Habukkuk back to his own place.

On the seventh day the king came to mourn for Daniel. As he came to the den and looked in, there was Daniel sitting there. The king cried aloud, "You are great, O Lord, the God of Daniel, and there is no other besides you!" He brought Daniel out, but those who had tried to destroy him he threw into the den, and they were devoured in a moment before his eyes. Daniel 14:28-42

Daniel is in dire straights; he has been cast into the lions den. Since the den was sealed no one knows what happened except God and Daniel. Hungry lions do not trample and eat Daniel as they normally would have. When Daniel is removed from the lions den and his accusers thrown in with their families they are immediately devoured. God closed the mouths of lions so that Daniel might survive. This was a miracle.

# EXPULSING DEMONS

When he came to the other side, to the territory of the Gadarenes, two demoniacs who were coming from the tombs met him. They were so savage that no one could travel by that road. They cried out, "What have you to do with us , Son of God? Have you come here to torment us before the appointed time?" Some distance away a herd of many swine was feeding. The demons pleaded with him, "If you drive us out, send us into the herd of swine." And he said to them, "Go then!" They came out and entered the swine, and the whole herd rushed down the steep bank into the sea where they drowned. The swineherds ran away, and when they came to the town they reported everything, including what had happened to the demoniacs. Thereupon the whole town came out to meet Jesus, and when they saw him they begged him to leave their district. Matthew 8:8-34

Then Jesus went from that place and withdrew to the region of Tyre and Sidon. And behold, a Canaanite woman of that district came and called out, "Have pity on me Lord, Son of David! My daughter is tormented by a demon." But he did not say a word in answer to her. His disciples came and asked him, "Send her away, for she keeps calling out after us." He said in reply, "I was sent only to the lost sheep of the house of Israel." But the woman came and did him homage, saying, "Lord, help me." He said in reply, "It is not right to take the food of the children and throw it to the dogs." She said, "Please, Lord, for even the dogs eat the scraps that fall from the table of their masters." Then Jesus said to her in reply, "O woman, great is your faith! Let it be done for you as you wish." And her daughter was healed from that hour. Matthew 15:21-28

When they came to the crowd a man approached, knelt down before him, and said, "Lord, have pity on my son, for he is a lunatic and suffers severely; often he falls into fire, and often into water. I brought him to your disciples, but they could not cure him." Jesus said in reply, "O faithless and perverse generation , how long will I be with you? How long will I endure you? Bring him here to me." Jesus rebuked him and the demon came out of him, and from that hour the boy was cured. Then the disciples approached Jesus in private and said, "Why could we not drive it out?" He said to them, "Because of your little faith. Amen, I say to you, if you have the faith the size of a mustard seed, you will say to this mountain , 'Move from here to there,' and it will move. Nothing will be impossible for you." Matthew 17:14-21

Then they came to Capernaum, and on the sabbath he entered the synagogue and taught. The people were astonished at his teaching, for he taught them as one having authority and not as the scribes. In their synagogue was a man with an unclean spirit; he cried out, "What have you to do with us, Jesus of Nazareth? Have you come to destroy us? I know who you are—the Holy one of God!" Jesus rebuked him and said, "Quiet! Come out of him!" The unclean spirit convulsed him and with a loud cry came out of him. All were amazed and asked one another , "What is this? A new teaching with authority. He commands even the unclean spirits and they obey him." His fame spread everywhere throughout the whole region of Galilee. Mark 1:21-28

They came to the other side of the sea, to the territory of the Gerasenes. When he got out of the boat, at once a man from the tombs who had an unclean spirit met him. The man had ben dwelling among the tombs, and no one could restrain him any longer, even with a chain. In fact, he had frequently been bound with shackles and chains, but the chains had been pulled apart by him and the shackles smashed, and no one was strong enough to subdue him. Night and day among the tombs and on the hillsides he was always crying out and bruising himself with stones. Catching sight of Jesus from a distance, he ran up and prostrated himself before him, crying out in a loud voice, "What have you to do with me , Jesus, Son of the Most High God? I adjure `you by God, do not torment me!" (He had been saying to him, "Unclean spirit, come out of the man!") He asked him, "What is your name?" He replied, "Legion is my name. There are many of us." And he pleaded earnestly with him not to drive them away from that territory.

Now a large herd of swine was feeding there on the hillside. And they pleaded with him, "Send us into the swine. Let us enter them." And he let them , and the unclean spirits came out and entered the swine. The herd of about two thousand rushed down a steep bank into the sea, where they were drowned. The swine herds ran away and reported the incident in the town and throughout the countryside And people came out to see what had happened. As they approached Jesus, they caught sight of the man who had been possessed by Legion, sitting there clothed and in his right mind. And they were seized with fear. Those who witnessed the incident explained to them what had happened to the possessed man and to the swine. They then began to beg him to leave their district. As he was getting into the boat, the man who had been possessed pleaded to remain with him. But he would not permit him but told him instead, "Go home to your family and announce to them all that the Lord in his pity has done for you." Then the man went off and began to proclaim in the Decapolis what Jesus had done for him; and all were amazed. Mark 5:1—20

From that place he went off to the district of Tyre. He entered a house and wanted no one to know about it, but he could not escape notice. Soon a woman whose daughter had an unclean spirit heard about him. She came and fell at his feet. The woman was a Greek, a Syrophoenician by birth, and she begged him to drive the demon out of her daughter. He said to her, "Let the children be fed first. For it is not right to take the food of the children and throw it to the dogs." She replied and said to him, "Lord, even the dogs under the table eat the children's scraps." Then he said to her, "For saying this you may go. The demon has gone out of your daughter." When the woman went home, she found the child lying in bed and the demon gone. Mark 7:24-30

When they came to the disciples, they say a large crowd around them and the scribes arguing with them. Immediately on seeing him, the whole crowd was utterly amazed. They ran up and greeted him. He asked them, "What are you arguing about with them?" Someone from the crowd answered him, "Teacher, I have brought to you my son possessed by a mute spirit. Whenever it seizes him, it throws him down; he foams at the mouth, grinds his teeth, and becomes rigid. I asked your disciples to drive it out, but they were unable to do so." He said to them in reply, "O faithless generation, how long will I be with you? How long will I endure you? Bring him to me." They brought the boy to him. And, when he saw him, the spirit immediately threw the boy into convulsions. As he fell to the ground, he began to roll around and foam at the mouth. Then he questioned his father, "How long has this been happening to him?" He replied, "Since childhood. It has often thrown him into fire and into water to kill him. But if you can do anything, have compassion on us and help us." Jesus said to him, "'If you can!' Everything is possible to one who has faith." Then the boy's father cried out, "I do believe, help my unbelief!" Jesus, on seeing a crowd rapidly gathering, rebuked the unclean spirit and said to it, "Mute and deaf spirit, I command you: come out of him and never enter him again!" Shouting and throwing the boy into convulsions, it came out. He became like a corpse, which caused many to say, "He is dead!" But Jesus took him by the hand, raised him, and he stood up. When he entered the house, his disciples asked him in private, "Why could we not drive it out?" He said to them, "This kind can only come out through prayer." Mark 9:14-29

Jesus then went down to Capernaum, a town of Galilee. He taught them on the sabbath, and they were astonished at his teaching because he spoke with authority. In the synagogue there was a man with the spirit of an unclean demon and he cried out in a loud voice, "Ha! What have you to do with us, Jesus of Nazareth? Have you come to destroy us? I know who you are—the Holy One of God!" Jesus rebuked him and said, " Be quiet! Come out of him!" Then the demon threw the man down in front of them and came out of him without doing him any harm. They were all amazed and said to one another, "What is there about his word? For with authority and power he commands the unclean spirits, and they come out." And news of him spread everywhere in the surrounding region. Luke 4:31-37

And demons also came out from many, shouting, "You are the son of God." But he rebuked them and did not allow thwm to speak because he knew he was the Messiah. Luke 4:41

Then they sailed to the territory of the Gerasenes, which is opposite Galilee. When he came ashore a man from the town who was possessed by demons met him. For a long time he had not worn clothes; he did not live in a house, but lived among the tombs. When he saw Jesus, he cried out and fell down before him; in a loud voice he shouted, "What have you to do with me, Jesus, Son of the Most High God? I beg you, do not torment me!" For he had ordered the unclean spirit to come out of the man. (It had taken hold of him many times, and he used to be bound with chains and shackles as a restraint, but he would break his bonds and be driven by the demon into deserted places.) The Jesus asked him, "What is your name?" He replied, "Legion" because many demons had entered him. And they pleaded with him not to order them to depart to the abyss.

A herd of many swine was feeding there on the hillside, and they pleaded with him to allow them to enter those swine; and he let them. The demons came out of the man and entered the swine, and the herd rushed down the steep bank into the lake and was drowned. When the swineherds saw what had happened, they ran away and reported the incident in the town and throughout the countryside. People came out to see what had happened and, when they approached Jesus, they discovered the man from whom the demons had come out sitting at his feet. He was clothed and in his right mind, and they were seized with fear. Those who witnessed it told them how the possessed man had been saved. The entire population of the region of the Gerasenes asked Jesus to leave them because they were seized with great fear. So he got into a boat and returned. The man from whom the demons had come out begged to remain with him, but he sent him away, saying, "Return home and recount what God has done for you." The man went off and proclaimed throughout the whole town what Jesus had done for him. Luke 8:26-38

On the next day, when they came down from the mountain, a large crowd met him. There was a man in the crowd who cried out, "Teacher, I beg you, look at my son; he is my only child. For a spirit seizes him and he suddenly screams and it convulses him until he foams at the mouth; it releases him only with difficulty, wearing him out, I begged your disciples to cast it out but they could not." Jesus said in reply, " O faithless and perverse generation, how long will I be with you and endure you? Bring your son here." AS he was coming forward, the demon threw him to the ground in a convulsion; but Jesus rebuked the unclean spirit, healed the boy, and returned him to his father. And all were astonished by the majesty of God. Luke 9:37-43

We don't hear much today of demon possessed people. We do hear of devil worshippers, witches, warlocks and people who commit grave evils. In Jesus day there were many who were possessed by evil spirits and Jesus, as exorcist, expulsed them. Exorcists exist today to remove evil spirits from people. One of the miracles of God was in the Book of Tobit where the evil demon Asmodeus is expulsed from Sarah. The real miracle of the expulsion of demons is God's power to remove evil spirits from people saving them from evil and sin.

# MIRACLES - UP TO HEAVEN

When Enoch was sixty-five years old, he begot Methuselah. Enoch walked with God after he begot Methuselah for three hundred years, and he had other sons and daughters. The whole lifetime of Enoch was three hundred and sixty five years. Enoch walked with God, and he was no longer here for God took him. Genesis 5:21-24

When the LORD was about to take Elijah up to heaven in a whirlwind, he and Elisha were on their way from Gilgal. 2 Kings 2:!

When they had crossed over, Elijah said to Elisha, "Request whatever I might do to you, before I am taken from you." Elisha answered, "May I receive a double portion of your spirit." He replied, "You have asked something that is not easy. Still, if you see me taken up from you, your wish will be granter; otherwise not." As they walked on still conversing, a fiery chariot and fiery horses came between the two of them, and Elijah went up to heaven in a whirlwind, and Elisha saw it happen. He cried out, "My father! My Father! Israel's chariot and steeds!"" Then he saw him no longer. 2 Kings 2:9-12

Four people are mentioned in the bible as ascending directly to heaven at the end of their earthly lives. These include Enoch, Elijah, Jesus, and Jesus's mother Mary. Elijah's ascent to heaven was witnessed by Elisha and Jesus's ascension by over five hundred people. It is a miracle for somebody to be taken directly up to heaven though all believers will be at the end of the age.

## MIRACLES—HARD TO BELIEVE

God said to Noah and to this sons with him: See, I am now establishing my covenant with you and your descendants after you and with every living creature that was with you: the birds, the tame animals, and all the wild animals that were with you- all that came out of the ark. I will establish my covenant with you, that never again shall all creatures be destroyed by waters of a flood; there shall not be another flood to devastate the earth. God said: This is the sign of the covenant that I am making between me and you and every living creature with you for all ages to come: I set my bow in the clouds to serve as a sign of the covenant between me and the earth. When I bring clouds over the earth, and the bow appears in the clouds. I will remember my covenant between me and you and every living creature—every mortal being—

*Some of God's Miracles*

so that the waters will never again become a flood to destroy every mortal being. When the bow appears in the clouds, I will see it and remember the covenant between God and every living creature—every mortal being that is on earth. God told Noah: This is a sign of the covenant I have established between me and every mortal being that is on earth Genesis 9:8-17

Then the LORD said to Moses: I am going to rain down bread from heaven for you. Each day the people are to go out and gather their daily portion; thus I will test them, to see whether they follow my instructions or not. ON the sixth day, however, when they prepare what they bring in, let it be twice as much as they gather on the other days. So Moses and Aaron told all the Israelites, "At evening you will know that it was the LORD who brought you out of the land of Egypt; and in the morning you will see the glory of the LORD, when he hears your grumbling against him. But who are we that you should grumble against us?" And Moses said, "When the LORD gives you meat to eat in the evening and in the morning your fill of bread, and hears the grumbling you utter against him, who then are we? Your grumbling is not against us, but against the LORD."

Then Moses said to Aaron, "Tell the whole Israelite community: approach the LORD, for he has heard your grumbling." But while Aaron was speaking to the whole Israelite community, they turned in the direction of the wilderness, and there the glory of the LORD appeared in the cloud! The LORD said to Moses: I have heard the grumbling of the Israelites. Tell them :In the evening twilight you will eat meat, and in the morning you will have your fill of bread, and then you will know that I, the LORD, am your God.

In the evening, quail came up and covered the camp. In the morning there was a layer of dew all about the camp, and when the layer of dew evaporated, fine flakes were on the surface of the wilderness, fine flakes like hoarfrost on the ground. On seeing it, the Israelites asked one another, "What is this?" for they did not know what it was. But Moses told them, It is the bread which the LORD has given you to eat.

"Now, this is what the LORD has commanded. Gather as much of it as each needs to eat, an omer for each person for as many of you as there are, each of you providing for those in your own tent." The Israelites did so. Some gathered a large and some a small amount. But when they measured it out by the omer, the one who had gathered a large amount did not have too much, and the one who had gathered a small amount did not have too little. They gathered as much as they needed to eat. Moses said to them, "Let no one leave any of it over until morning." But they did not listen to Moses, and some kept a part of it over until morning, and it became wormy and stank. Therefore Moses was angry with them.

Morning after morning they gathered it, as much as they needed to eat; but when the sun grew hot, it melted away. On the sixth day they gathered twice as much food, two omers for each person. When all the leaders of the community came and reported this to Moses, he told them, "That is what the LORD has prescribed. Tomorrow is a day of rest, a holy sabbath of the LORD. Whatever you want to bake, bake; whatever you want to boil, boil; but whatever is left put away and keep until the morning." When they put it away until the morning, as Moses commanded, it did not stink nor were there worms in it. Moses then said, "Eat it today for today is the sabbath of the LORD. Today you will not find any in the field. Six days you will gather it, but on the seventh day, the sabbath, it will not be there." Still, on the seventh day some of the people went out to gather it, but they did not find any. Then the LORD said to Moses: How long will you refuse to keep my commandments and my instructions? Take note! The LORD has given you the sabbath. That is why on the sixth day he gives you food for two days. Each of you stay where you are and let no one go out on the seventh day. After that the people rested on the seventh day.

The house of Israel named this food manna. It was like coriander seed, white, and it tasted like wafers made from honey.

Moses said, "This is what the LORD has commanded. Keep a full omer of it for your future generations, so that they may see the food I gave you to eat in the wilderness when I brought you out of the land of Egypt." Moses then told Aaron, "Take a jar and put a full omer of manna in it. Then place it before the LORD to keep it for your future generations." As the LORD had commanded Moses, Aaron placed it in front of the covenant to keep it.

The Israelites ate the manna for forty years, until they ame to settled land; they ate the manna until they came to the borders of Canaan. (An omer is one tenth of an ephah.) Exodus 16:4-36

Hundreds of thousands of people were fed in the Sinai desert and ate manna which was found on the ground. This heavenly food was provided and is in fact a miracle.

When Elisha returned to Gilgal, there was a famine in the land. Once, when the guild prophets were seated before him, he said to his servant, "Put the large pot on, and make some vegetable stew for the guild prophets." Some-one went into the field to gather herbs and fond a wild vine, from which he picked a sackful of poisonous wild gourds. On his return he cut them up into the pot of vegetable stew without anybody's knowing it. The stew was served, but when they began to eat it, they cried, "Man of God, there is death in this pot!" And they could not eat it. He said, "Bring some meal." He threw it into the pot and said, "Serve it to the people to eat." And there was no longer anything harmful in the pot. 2 Kings 4:3a8-41

The change of poisonous food to food that people could eat was miracle.

The guild prophets once said to Elisha: "This place where we live with you is two cramped for us. Let us go to the Jordan, where by getting one beam apiece we can build ourselves a place to live." Elisha said, "Go". One of them requested, "Please agree to accompany your servants." He replied, "Yes, I will come."

So he went with them, and when they arrived at the Jordan they began to cut down trees. While one of them was felling a tree trunk, the iron ax blade slipped into the water. He cried out, "Oh, no master! It was borrowed!" "Where did it fall?" asked the man of God. When he pointed out the spot, Elisha cut off a stick, threw it into the water, and brought the iron to the surface. He said pick it up." And the man stretched out his hand and grasped it. 2 Kings 6:1-7

Perhaps the recovery of the ax blade could be explained if they had a giant magnet, but to pick up the ax head with only a stick is a miracle. Try it yourself!

When they came to Capernaum, the collectors of the temple tax approached Peter and said, "Doesn't your teacher pay the temple tax?" "Yes," he said. When he came into the house before he had time to speak, Jesus asked him, "What is your opinion, Simon? From whom do the kings of the earth takes tolls or census tax? From the subjects or from foreigners?" When he said, "From foreigners," Jesus said to him, "Then the subjects are exempt. But that we may not offend them, go to the sea, drop in a hook, and take the first fish that comes up. Open its mouth and you will find a coin worth twice the temple tax. Give that to them for me and for you." Matthew 17:-24-27

To recover a coin from the mouth of a randomly caught fish is a miracle and unheard of except in the gospel.

## POWER OVER WATER

The Angel of God who had been leading Israel's army, now moved and went around behind them. And the column of cloud, moving from in front of them, took up its place behind them, so that it came between the Egyptian army, and that of Israel. And when it became dark, the cloud illuminated the night; and so the rival camps did not come any closer together all night long. Then Moses stretched out his hand over the sea; and the LORD drove back the sea with a strong east wind all night long and turned the sea into dry ground. The waters were split, so that the Israelites entered into the midst of the sea on dry land, with the water as a wall to their right and to their left.

*Some of God's Miracles*

The Egyptians followed in pursuit of them—all Pharaoh's horses and chariots and horsemen—into the midst of the sea. But during the watch just before dawn, the LORD looked down from a column of fiery cloud upon the Egyptian army and threw it into a panic; and he so clogged their chariot wheels that they could drive only with difficulty. With that the Egyptians said, Let us flee from Israel, because the LORD is fighting for them against Egypt."

Then the LORD spoke to Moses: Stretch out your hand over the sea, that the water may flow back upon the Egyptians, upon their chariots and their horsemen. So Moses stretched out his hand over the sea, and at daybreak the sea returned to its normal flow. he Egyptians were fleeing head on toward it when the LORD cast the Egyptians into the midst of the sea. As the water flowed back, it covered the chariots and the horsemen. Of all Pharaoh's army which had followed the Israelites into the sea, not even one escaped. But the Israelites had walked on dry land through the midst of the sea, with the water as a wall to their right and to their left. Thus the LORD saved Israel on that day from the power of Egypt. When Israel saw the Egyptians lying dead on the seashore and saw the great power that the LORD had shown against

Egypt, the people feared the LORD. They believed in the LORD and in Moses his servant. Exodus 14:19-30

Water seeks its own level so to observe water divide itself so people can pass though is unheard of. This is especially true when it is done at the command of a human person. The separation of waters in the red sea so that the Israelites could pass was a miracle.

The ark of the covenant of the Lord of the whole earth will cross the Jordan before you. Now choose twelve men, one from each of the tribes of Israel. When the soles of the priests carrying the ark of the LORD, the Lord of the whole earth, touch the waters of the Jordan, it will cease to flow; the water flowing down from upstream will halt in a single heap."

The people set out from their tents to cross the Jordan, with the priests carrying the ark of the covenant ahead of them. When those bearing the ark came to the Jordan and the feet of the priests bearing the ark were immersed in the banks of the Jordan—which overflows all its banks during the entire season of the harvest—the waters flowing from upstream halted, standing in a single heap for a very great distance indeed, from Adam, a city in the direction of Zarethan; those flowing downstream towards the Salt

Sea of the Arabah disappeared entirely. Thus the people crossed over opposite Jericho. The priests carrying the ark of the covenant of the LORD stood on dry ground in the Jordan riverbed while all Israel crossed on dry ground, until the whole nation had completed the crossing of the Jordan.

After the entire nation had completed the crossing of the Jordan, the LORD said to Joshua: Choose twelve men from the people, one from each tribe, and command them, "Take up twelve stones from the spot in the Jordan riverbed where the priests have been standing. Carry them over with you, and place them where you are to stay tonight."

Summoning the twelve men he had selected from among the Israelites, one from each tribe , Joshua said to them: "Go to the Jordan riverbed in front of the ark of the LORD, you God; lift to your shoulders, one stone apiece, so that they will equal in number the tribes of the Israelites. In the future, these are to be a sign among you. When your children ask you, what do these stones mean to you?' You shall answer them, 'The waters of the Jordan ceased to flow before the ark of the covenant of the LORD when it crossed the Jordan.' Thus these stones are to serve as a perpetual memorial to the Israelites." The twelve

Israelites did as Joshua had commanded; they took up twelve stones from the Jordan Riverbed as the LORD had said to Joshua, one for each of the tribes of the Israelites. They carried them along to the camp site, and there they placed them. Joshua set up the twelve stones that had been in the Jordan riverbed on the spot where the priests stood who were carrying the ark of the covenant. They are there to this day.

The priests carrying the ark stood in the Jordan riverbed until everything had been done that the LORD had commanded Joshua to tell the people, just as Moses had commanded Joshua. The people crossed over quickly, and when all the people had completed the crossing, the ark of the LORD also crossed; and the priests were now in front of them. The Reubenites, Gadites, and half tribe of Manasseh, armed, marched in the vanguard of the Israelites, as Moses had ordered. About forty thousand troops, equipped for battle, crossed over before the LORD to the plains of Jericho for war.

That day the LORD exalted Joshua in the site of all Israel, and so during his whole life they feared him as they had feared Moses.

*Some of God's Miracles*

Then the lord said to Joshua: Command the priests carrying the ark of the covenant to come up from the Jordan. Joshua commanded the priests, "Come up from the Jordan." And when the priests carrying the ark of the covenant of the LORD had come up from the Jordan riverbed, as the soles of their feet regained the dry ground, the waters of the Jordan resumed their course and as before overflowed all its banks.

The people came up from the Jordan on the tenth day of the first month, and camped in Gilgal on the eastern limits of Jericho. At Gilgal Joshua set up the twelve stones that had been taken from the Jordan, saying to the Israelites, "In the future, when your children ask their parents, 'What do these stones mean?' You shall inform them, 'Israel crossed the Jordan here on dry ground.' For the LORD, your God, dried up the waters of the Jordan in front of you until you crossed over, just as the LORD, your God, had done at the Red Sea, drying it up in front of us until we crossed over, in order that all the peoples of the earth may know that that hand of the LORD is mighty, and that you may fear the LORD, your God forever. Joshua 3:11-4:24

For water to stop flowing in a river and back up while people cross on dry land is a miracle and unheard of except in this context.

He got into a boat and his disciples followed him. Suddenly a violent storm came up on the sea, so that the boat was being swamped by waves; but he was asleep. They came and woke him, saying, "Lord, save us! WE are perishing!" He said to them, "Why are you terrified, O you of little faith?" Then he got up rebuked the winds and the sea, and there was great calm. The men were amazed and said, "What sort of man is this, whom even the winds and sea obey?" Matthew 8:23-27

On that day, as evening drew on, he said to them, "Let us cross over to the other side." Leaving the crowd, they took him with them in the boat just as he was. And other boats were with him. A violent squall came up and waves were breaking over the boat, so that it was already filling up. Jesus was in the stern, asleep on a cushion. They woke him and said to him, "Teacher do you not care that we are perishing?" He woke up, rebuked the wind, and said to the sea, "Quiet! Be still!" The wind ceased and there was great calm. Then he asked them, "Why are you terrified? Do you not yet have faith?" They were filed with great awe and said to one another, "Who then is this whom even the wind and sea obey?" Mark 4:35-41

One day he got into a boat with his disciples and said to them, "Let us go to the other side of the lake." So they set sail, and while they were sailing he fell asleep. A squall blew over the lake, and they were taking in water and they were in danger. They came and woke him saying, "Master, master, we are perishing !!!" He awakened, rebuked the wind and the waves, and they subsided and these was a calm. He then asked them, "Where is your faith?" But they were filled with awe and amazed and said to one another, "Who then is this, who commands even the winds and the sea, and they obey him?" Luke 8:22-25

Then he made the disciples get into the boat and precede him to the other side, while he dismissed the crows. After doing so, he went up on the mountain by himself to pray. When it was evening he was there alone. Meanwhile the boat, already a few miles offshore, was being tossed about by the waves, for the wind was against it. During the forth watch of the night, he came toward them, walking on the sea. When the disciples saw him walking on the sea they were terrified. "It is a ghost," they said, and they cried out in fear. At once [Jesus] spoke to them, "Take courage, it is I; do not be afraid." Peter said to him in reply, "Lord, if it is you, command me to come to you on the water." He said, "Come." Peter got out of the boat and began to walk on the water towards Jesus. But when he saw how [strong] the wind was he became frightened; and beginning to sink, he cried out, "Lord, save me!" Immediately Jesus stretched out his hand and caught him, and said to him "O you of little faith, why did you doubt?" after they got into the boat, the wind died down. Those who were in the boat did him homage, saying, "Truly you are the Son of God." Matthew 14:22-33

Then he made his disciples get into the boat and precede him to the other side toward Bethsaida, while he dismissed the crowd. And when he had taken leave of them, he went off to the mountain to pray. When it was evening, the boat was far out on the sea and he was alone on the shore. Then he saw that that they were tossed about while rowing, for the wind was against them. About the fourth watch f the night, he came toward them walking on the sea. He meant to pass by them. But when they saw him walking on the sea, they thought it was a ghost and cried out. They had all seen him and were terrified. But at once he spoke with them, "Take courage, it is I, do not be afraid!" He got into the boat with them and the wind died down. They were [completely] astounded. They had not understood the incident of the loaves. On the contrary their hearts were hardened. Mark6:45-52

When it was evening, his disciples went down to the sea, embarked in a boat, and went across the sea to Capernaum. It had already grown dark, and Jesus had not yet come to them. The sea was stirred up because a strong wind was blowing. When they had rowed about three or four miles, they saw Jesus walking on the sea and coming near the boat, and they began to be afraid. But he said to them, "It is I. Do not be afraid." They wanted to take him into the boat, but the boat immediately arrived at the shore to which they were heading. John 616-21

Jesus walked on water though this is impossible he also calmed the storm showing that he had power over nature.

On the third day there was a wedding in Cana in Galilee and the mother of Jesus was there, Jesus and his disciples were also invited to the wedding. When the wine ran short, the mother of Jesus said to him, "They have no wine." [And} Jesus said to her, "Woman, how does your concern affect me? My hour has not yet come." His mother said to the servers, "Do whatever he tells you." Now there were six stone water jars there for Jewish ceremonial washing, each holding twenty to thirty gallons. Jesus told them, "Fill the jars with water." So they filled them to the brim. Them he told them, "Draw some out now and take it to the headwaiter." SO they took it. And when the headwaiter tasted the water that had become wine, without knowing where it came from (Although the servers who had drawn the water knew), the headwaiter called the bridegroom, and said to him, "everyone serves good wine first, and then when people have drunk freely, an inferior one; but you have kept the good wine until now." Jesus did this as the beginning of his signs in Cana in Galilee and so revealed his glory, and his disciples began to believe in him. John 2:1-11

Wine is made from grapes, sugar, yeast and water. It is unheard of that anyone could make wine out of plain water. It is clearly a miracle.

## MIRACLES IN FIRE

King Nebuchadnezzar had a golden statue made, sixty cubits high and six cubits wide, which he set up in the plain of Dura in the province of Babylon. He then ordered the satraps, prefects, and governors, the counselors, treasurers, judges, magistrates and all the officials of the provinces to be summoned to the dedication of the statue which he had set up. The satraps, prefects, and governors, the counselors, treasurers, judges, magistrates and all the officials of the provinces came together for the dedication and stood before the statue which king Nebuchadnezzar had set up. A herald cried out: "Nations and peoples of every language, when you hear the sound of the horn, pipe, zither, dulcimer, harp, double flute, and all the other musical instruments, you must fall down and worship the golden statue which king Nebuchadnezzar has set up. Whoever does not fall down and worship shall be instantly cast into a white hot furnace." Therefore, as soon as they heard the sound of the horn, pipe zither, dulcimer, harp, double flute, and all the other musical instruments, the nations and peoples of every language all fell down and worshiped the golden statue which king Nebuchadnezzar had set up.

At that point, some of the Chaldeans came and accused the Jews to King Nebuchadnezzar: "O king, live forever! O king you issued a decree that everyone who heard the sound of the horn, pipe, zither, dulcimer, harp, and double flute, and all the other musical instruments should fall down and worship the golden statue; whoever did not was to be cast into a white-hot furnace. There are certain Jews whom you have made administrators of the province of Babylon: Shadrach, Meshach, and Abednego; these men, O king, have paid no attention to you ; they will not serve your god or worship the golden statue which you set up."

Nebuchadnezzar flew into a rage and sent for Shadrach, Meshach, and Abednego, who were promptly brought before the king. King Nebuchadnezzar questioned them: Is it true, Shadrach, Meshach, and Abednego, that you will not serve my god, or worship the statue that I made? Now, if you are ready to fall down and worship the statue I made, whenever you hear the sound of the horn, pipe, zither, dulcimer, harp, double flute, and all the other musical instruments, then all will be well; if not, you shall be instantly cast into the white-hot furnace; and who is the God that can deliver you out of my hands?" Shadrach, Meshach, and Abednego answered king Nebuchadnezzar, "There is no need for us to defend ourselves before you in this matter. If our God, whom we serve, can save us from the white-hot furnace and from your hands, O king, may he save us! But even if he will not, you should know, O king, that we will not serve your god or worship the golden statue which you set up."

Nebuchadnezzar's face became livid with utter rage against Shadrach, Meshach, and Abednego. He ordered the furnace to be heated seven times more than usual and had some of the strongest men in his army bind Shadrach, Meshach, and Abednego and cast them in the white-hot furnace. They were bound and cast into the white-hot furnace with their trousers, shirts, hats and other garments, for the king's order was urgent. So huge a fire was kindled in the furnace that the flames devoured the men who through Shadrach, Meshach, and Abednego into it. But these three fell, bound, into the midst of the white hot furnace. Daniel 3:1-23

Now the king's servants who had thrown them in continued to stoke the furnace with naphtha, pitch, tow, and brush. The flames rose forty-nine cubits above the furnace, and spread out, burning the Chaldeans that it caught around the furnace. But the angel of the Lord went down into the furnace with Azariah and his companions, drove the fiery flames out of the furnace as though a dew-laden breeze were blowing through it. The fire in no way touched them or caused them pain or harm. Then these three in the furnace with one voice sang, glorifying and blessing God. Daniel 3:46-51

Then King Nebuchadnezzar was startled and rose in haste , asking his counselors, "Did we not cast three men bound into the fire?" "Certainly, O king." they answered. "But," he replied, "I see four men unbound and unhurt, walking in the fire, and the fourth looks like a son of God." Then Nebuchadnezzar came to the opening of the white -hot furnace and called: "Shadrach, Meshach, and Abednego servants of the most high God, come out." Thereupon, Shadrach, Meshach, and Abednego came out of the fire. When the satraps, prefects, governors, and counselors of the king came together, they saw that the fire had had no power over the bodies of these men; not a hair of their heads had been singed, nor were their garments altered; there was not even a smell of fire about them. Nebuchadnezzar exclaimed, "Blessed be the God of Shadrach, Meshach, and Abednego, who sent his angel to deliver the servants who trusted in him; they disobeyed the royal command and yielded their bodies rather than serve or worship any god except their own God. Therefore I decree for nations and peoples of every language that whoever blasphemes the God of Shadrach, Meshach, and Abednego shall be cut to pieces and his house made into a refuse heap. For there is no other God who can rescue like this." Then the king promoted Shadrach, Meshach, and Abednego in the province of Babylon. Daniel 3:91-100

Three Jewish men who did not want to offend God by serving or worshiping a golden statue and the Babylonian god of Nebuchadnezzar risked death by fire. At the king's order these three men were cast into a white hot furnace that devoured the soldiers who threw them in. Had it been any other situation the fire would have burned these three men to a crisp and then smoke and ashes. God protected the men from the fire so that they remained untouched by the fire. God intervened powerfully to save the three men. This might serve as an example in modern day life when we are thrown in "social infernos" for not obeying modern day god's such as materialism. When we obey God alone and worship him alone we can be sure of the salvation of God if we lead holy lives. Like Daniel in the Lions Den, or David when king Saul wanted to kill him, or Lot leaving Sodom and Gomorrah we can be sure of God's saving hand. The miracle of the fiery furnace is that it is impossible to be protected from fire when thrown into a white-hot furnace yet this is exactly what God did. Contrast this with the soldiers who threw these men in and obeyed Nebuchadnezzar: They were immediately consumed by the flames.

# BABIES FROM DEAD WOMBS

The Lord appeared to Abraham by the oak of Mamre, as he sat in the entrance of his tent, while the day was growing hot. Looking up, he saw three men standing near him. When he saw them, he ran from the entrance of the tent to greet them; and bowing to the ground, he said: "Sir, if it please you, do not go on past your servant. Let some water be brought, that you may bathe your feet, and then rest under the tree. Now that you have come to your servant, let me bring you a little food, that you may refresh yourselves; and afterward you may go on your way." "Very well," they replied, "do as you have said."

Abraham hurried into the tent to Sarah and said, "Quick, three measures of bran flour! Knead it and make bread." He ran to the herd, picked out a tender, choice calf, and gave t to a servant, who quickly prepared it. Then he got some curds and milk, as well as the calf that had been prepared, and set these before them, waiting on them under the tree while they ate.

"Where is your wife Sarah?" they asked him. "There in the tent," he replied. One of them said, " I will return to you about the same time next year, and Sarah will then have a son." Sarah was listening at the entrance of the tent, just behind him. Now Abraham and Sarah were old, advanced in years, and Sarah had stopped having her menstrual periods. So Sarah laughed to herself and said, "Now that I am worn out and my husband is old, am I still to have sexual pleasure?" But the LORD said to Abraham: "Why did Sarah laugh and say, "Will I really bearca child, old as I am? Is anything too marvelous for the LORD to do? At the appointed time , about this time next year, I will return to you, and Sarah will have a son." Sarah lied, saying, "I did not laugh," because she was afraid. But he said, "Yes you did." Genesis 18:1-15

The LORD took note of Sarah as he had said he would; the LORD did for her as he had promised. Sarah became pregnant and bore Abraham a son in his old age, at the set time that God had stated. Abraham gave the name Isaac to this son of his whom Sarah bore him. When his son Isaac was eight days old, Abraham circumcised him, as God had commanded. Abraham was a hundred years old when his son Isaac was born to him. Sarah then said, "God has given me cause to laugh, and all who hear it will laugh with me. Who would ever have told Abraham," she added, "that Sarah would nurse children! Yet I have borne him a son in his old age." The child grew and was weaned, and Abraham held a great banquet on the day of the child's weaning. Genesis 21:1-8

There was a certain man from Ramathaim, a Zuphite from the hill country of Ephraim. His name was Elkanah, the son of Jeroham, son of Elihu, son of Tohu, son of Zuph, an Ephraimite. He had two wives, one named Hannah, the other Peninnah; Peninnah had children, but Hannah had no children. Each year this man went up from his city to worship and offer sacrifice to the LORD of hosts at Shiloh, where the two sons of Eli, Hophni and Phinehas, were ministering as priests of the LORD. When the day came for Elkanah to offer sacrifice, he used to give portions to his wife Peninnah and to all her sons and daughters, but he would give a double portion to Hannah because he loved her, though the LORD had closed her womb. Her rival, to upset her, would torment her constantly, since the LORD had closed her womb.

Year after year, when she went up to the house of the LORD, Peninnah would provoke her, and Hannah would weep and refuse to eat. ELkanah, her husband, would say to her, "Hannah, why are you weeping? Why are you not eating? Why are you so miserable? AM I not better for you than ten sons?"

Hannah rose after one such meal at Shiloh, and presented herself before the LORD; at the time, Eli the priest was sitting on a chair near the doorpost of the LORD's temple. In her bitterness she prayed to the LORD, weeping copiously, and she made a vow promising: O LORD of hosts, if you look with pity on the misery of your handmaid, if you remember me and do not forget me, if you give your handmaid a male child, I will give him to the LORD for as long as he lives; neither wine nor liquor shall he drink, and no razor shall ever touch his head." As she remained long at prayer before the LORD. Eli watched her mouth, for Hannah was praying silently; though her lips were moving, her voice could not be heard. Eli, thinking she was drunk, said to her, "How long will you make a drunken spectacle of yourself? Sober up from your wine!" "No my Lord!" Hannah answered. "I am an unhappy woman. I have had neither wine nor liquor; I was only pouring out my heart to the LORD. Do not think your servant a worthless woman; my prayer has been prompted by deep sorrow and misery." Eli said, "Go in peace, and may the God of Israel grant what you have requested." She replied, "Let your servant find favor in your eyes," and left. She went to her quarters, ate and drank with her husband, and no longer appeared downhearted. Early the next morning they worshipped before the LORD, and then returned to their home in Ramah. When they returned Elkanah had intercourse with his wife Hannah, and the LORD remembered her.

She conceived and, at the end of her pregnancy, bore a son whom she named Samuel. "Because I asked the LORD for him." The next time her husband Elkanah was going up with the rest of his household to offer the customary sacrifice to the LORD and fulfill his vows, Hannah did not go, explaining to her husband, "Once the child is weaned, I will take him to appear before the LORD and leave him there forever. Her husband Elkanah answered her: "Do what you think best; wait until you have weaned him. Only may the LORD fulfill his word!" And so she remained at nursed her son until she had weaned him. 1 Samuel 9-23

Meanwhile the boy Samuel, wearing a linen ephod, was serving in the presence of the LORD. His mother used to make little garment for him, which she would bring him each time she went up with her husband to offer the customary sacrifice. And Eli would bless ELkanah and his wife, as they were leaving for home. He would say, " Mat the LORD repay you with children from this woman for the gift she has made to the LORD!" The LORD favored Hannah so that she conceived and gave birth to three more sons and two daughters, while young Samuel grew up in the service of the LORD. Samuel 218-21

One day Elisha came to Shunem, where there was a woman of influence, who pressed him to dine with her. Afterward, whenever he passed by, he would stop there to dine. So she said to her husband, "I know that he is a holy man of God. Since he visits us often, let us arrange a little room on the roof and furnish it for him with a bed, table, chair, and lamp so that when he comes to us he can stay there."

One day Elisha arrived and stayed in the room overnight. Then he said to his servant Gehazi, "Call the shunammite woman." He did so and when she stood before Elisha , he told Gehazi, "Say to her, 'You have troubled yourself greatly for us; what can we do for you? Can we say a good word for you to the king or to the commander of the army/" She replied, "I am living among my own people." Later Elisha asked, "What can we do for her?" Gehazi answered, "She has no son, and her husband is old." Elisha said, " Call her." He did so, and when she stood at the door, Elisha promised, "This time next year you will be cradling a baby son." She said, "My lord, you are a man of God; do not deceive your servant." Yet the woman conceived, and by the same time the following year she had given birth to a son as Elisha had promised; and the child grew up healthy. 2 Kings 4:8-17

And behold, Elizabeth, your relative, has also conceived a son in her old age, and this is the sixth month for her who was called barren; for nothing will be impossible for God. Luke 1:36-38

The old and new testament contain accounts of woman who were unable to bear children. In the book of Genesis, Abraham's wife Sarah does not bear a child until forty years after she would normally become officially sterile in her menopause. God, according to his promise to Abraham allows Sarah to bear Isaac in her old age. For is anything too marvelous for the LORD to do. Through Isaac Abraham begets descendants as numerous as the stars of the heavens and the sand of the seashore. Samuel's mother was also sterile but she implored the LORD and was blessed by a child. It is notable that Samuel's mother prayed for a child and was given one. Prayer is an important component for the realization of a miracle as is faith. Elisha is cared for by the Shunammite woman and miraculously predicts she will bear a son.. Mary's relative Elizabeth who is past the age for having children finds herself pregnant and bears John the Baptist. All these women who are either infertile or past the age of bearing children do bear children through God's miracles, for nothing will be impossible for God.

# RAISING THE DEAD

One day the boy went out to his father among the reapers. He said to his father, "My head! My head!" And his father said to the servant, "Carry him to his mother." The servant picked him up and carried him to his mother; he sat in her lap until noon, and then died. She went upstairs and laid him on the bed of the man of God. Closing the door on him, she went out and called to her husband,, "Let me have one of the servants and a donkey. I must go quickly to the man of God, and I will be back." He asked, "Why are you going to him today? It is neither the full moon nor the sabbath." But she said, "It is all right." When the donkey was saddled, she said to her servant, "Lead on! Do not stop my donkey unless I tell you." She kept going till she reached the man of God on Mount Carmel.. When he saw her at a distance, the man of God said to his servant Gehazi: "There is the

Shunammite! Hurry to meet her and ask her if everything is all right with her, and with her husband, and with the boy." "Everything is all right," she replied. But when she reached the man of God on the mountain, she clasped his feet. Gehazi came near to pusher away, but the man of God said: "Let her alone, she is in bitter anguish; the LORD hid it from me and did not let me know." She said, "Did I ask my lord for a son? Did I not say, 'Do not mislead me'? He said to Gehazi, "Get ready for a journey. Take my staff with you and be off; if you meet anyone, give no greeting , and if anyone greets you, do not answer. Lay my staff upon the boy." But the boy's mother cried out: "as the LORD lives and as you yourself live, I will not release you." So he started back with her.

Meanwhile, Gehazi had gone on ahead and had laid the staff upon the boy, but there was no sound, no response. He returned to meet Elisha and told him, "The boy has not awakened." When Elisha reached the house, he found the boy dead, lying on the bed. He went in, closed the door on the both, and prayed to the LORD. He then lay upon the child on the bed, placing his mouth upon the child's mouth, his eyes upon the eyes, and his hands upon the hands. As Elisha stretched himself over the child, the boy's flesh became warm. He arose, paced up and down the room, and then once more stretched himself over him, and the boy sneezed seven times and opened his eyes. Elisha summoned Gehazi and said, "Call the Shunammite." He called her, and she came to him, and Elisha said to her, "Take your son." She came in and fell at his feet in homage; then she took her son and left. 2 Kings 4:18-37

Soon afterward he journeyed to a city called Nain, and his disciples and a large crowd accompanied him. As he drew near to the gate of the city, a man who had died was being carried out, the only son of his mother, and she was a widow. A large crowd from the city was with her. When the Lord saw her, he was moved with pity for her and said to her, "Do not weep." He stepped forward and touched the coffin; at this the bearers halted, and he said, "Young man, I tell you arise!" and Jesus gave him to his mother. Fear seized them all, and they Glorified God, exclaiming, a great prophet has arisen in our midst," and God has visited his people. This report about him spread the whole of Judea and in all the surrounding region. Luke 7:11-17

While he was saying these thing to them, an official came forward, knelt down before him, and said, "My daughter has just died. But come, lay your hands upon her, and she will live." Jesus rose and followed him, and so did his disciples. A woman suffering hemorrhages for twelve years came up behind him and touched the tassel on his cloak. She said to herself, "If only I touch his cloak, I shall be cured." Jesus turned around and saw her, and said, "Courage daughter! Your faith has saved you." And from that hour the woman was saved.

When Jesus arrived at the officials house and saw the flute players and the crowd her were making a commotion, he said, "Go away! The girl is not dead but sleeping." And they ridiculed him. When the crowd was put out, he came and took her by the hand, and the little girl arose And news of this spread throughout all that land. Matthew 9:18-26

When Jesus had crossed again [in the boat] to the other side, a large crowd gathered around him, and he stayed close to the sea. One of the synagogue officials, named Jairus, came forward. Seeing him he fell at his feet and pleaded earnestly with him, saying, "My daughter is at the point of death. Please come lay your hands on her that she may get well and live." He went off with him, and a large crowd followed him and pressed upon him.

There was a woman afflicted with hemorrhages for twelve years. She had suffered greatly at the hands of many doctors and had spent all that she had. Yet she was not helped but only grew worse. She had heard about Jesus and came up behind him in the crowd and touched his cloak. She said, "If I but touch his clothes, I shall be cured." Immediately her flow of blood dried up. She felt in her body that she was healed of her affliction. Jesus, aware at once that power had gone out from him, turned around in the crowd and asked who has touched my clothes?" But his disciples said to him, "You see how thw crowd is pressing upon you, and yet you ask, 'Who touched me?'" And he looked around to see who had done it. The woman, realizing what had happened to her, approached in fear and trembling. She fell down before Jesus and told him the whole truth. He said to her, "Daughter, your faith has saved you. Go in peace and be cured of your affliction."

While he was still speaking, people from the synagogue official's house arrived and said, "Your daughter has died; why trouble the teacher any longer?" Disregarding the message that was reported, Jesus said to the synagogue official, Do not be afraid; just have faith." He did not allow anyone to accompany him inside except Peter, James, and John, the brother of James. When they arrived at the house of the synagogue official, he caught sight of a commotion, people weeping and wailing loudly. SO he went in and said to them, "Why this commotion and weeping? The child is not is not dead but asleep." And they ridiculed him. Then he put them all out. He took along the child's father and mother and those who were with him and entered the room where the child was. He took the child by the hand and said to her, "*Talitha koum*," which means, "Little girl, I say to you arise!" The girl, a child of twelve, arose immediately and walked around. [At that] they were utterly astounded. He gave strict orders that no one should know this and said that she should be given something to eat. Mark 5:21-43

When Jesus returned, the crowd welcomed him , for they were all waiting for him. And a man named Jairus, and official of the synagogue, came forward. He fell at the feet of Jesus and begged him to come to his house, because he had an only daughter, about twelve years old, and she was dying. As he went, the crowds almost crushed him. And a woman afflicted with hemorrhages for twelve years, who [had spent her whole livelihood on doctosr and was unable to be cured by anyone], came up behind him and touched the tassel on his cloak. Immediately her bleeding stopped. Jesus then asked, "Who touched me?" While all were denying it, Peter said, "Master, the crowds are pushing and pressing in upon you." But Jesus said, "Someone has touched me for I know that power has gone out from me." When the woman realized that she had not escaped notice, she came forward trembling. Falling down before him, she explained in the presence of all the people why she had touched him and how she had been healed immediately. He said to her, "Daughter, your faith has saved you go in peace."

While he was still speaking, someone from the synagogue official's house arrived and said, "Your daughter is dead; do not trouble the teacher any longer." On hearing this, Jesus answered him, "Do not be afraid; just have faith and she will be saved." When he arrived at the house he allowed no one to enter with him except Peter and John and James, and the child's father and mother. All were weeping and mourning for her, when he said, "Do not weep any longer, for she is not dead, but sleeping." And they ridiculed him, because they knew that she was dead. But he took her by the hand and called to her, "Child arise!" Her breath returned and she immediately arose. He then directed that she should be given something to eat. Her parents were astounded and he instructed them to tell no one what had happened. Luke 8:40-56

Now a man was ill, Lazarus from Bethany, the village of Mary and her sister Martha. Mary was the one who had anointed the Lord with perfumed oil and dried his feet with her hair; it was her brother Lazarus who was ill. So the sisters sent word to him, saying, "Master, the one you love is ill." When Jesus heard this he said, "This illness is not to end in , but for the Glory of God, that the Son of God may be glorified through it." Now Jesus loved Martha and her sister and Lazarus. So when he heard that he was ill, he remained for two days in the place where he was. Then after this he said to his disciples, "Let us go back to Judea." The disciples said to him, "Rabbi, the jews were just trying to stone you, and you want to go back there?" Jesus answered, "are there not twelve hours in a day? If one walks walks during the day he does not stumble, because he sees the light of this world. But if one walks at night, he stumbles, because the light is not in him. He said this, and then told them, "Our friend Lazarus is asleep, but I am going to awaken him." So the disciples said to him, "Master, if he is asleep, he will be saved." But Jesus was talking about his death, while they thought that he meant ordinary sleep. So them Jesus said to them clearly, "Lazarus has died. And. I am glad for you that I was not there, , that you may believe. Let us go to him," So Thomas, called Didymus, said to his fellow disciples, "let us also go to die with him."

When Jesus arrived, he found that Lazarus had already been in the tomb for four days. Now Bethany was near Jerusalem, only about two miles away. And many of the Jews had come to Martha and Mary to comfort them about their brother. When Martha heard that Jesus was coming, she went to meet him; but Mary sat at home. Martha said to Jesus, "Lord, if you had been here, my brother would not have died. [But] even now I know that whatever you ask of God, God will give you." Jesus said to her, "Your brother will rise." Martha said to him, "I know he will rise, in the resurrection on the last day," Jesus told her, "I am the resurrection and the life; who ever believes in me, even if he dies, will live, and everyone who lives and believes in me will never die. Do you believe this?" She said to him, "Yes, Lord. I have come to believe that you are the Messiah, the Son of God, the one who is coming into the world."

When she had said this, she went and called her sister Mary secretly saying, "The teacher is here and is asking for you." As soon as she heard this, she rose quickly and went to him. For Jesus had not yet come into the village,. But was still where Martha had met him. So when the Jews who were with her in the house comforting her saw Mary get up quickly and go out, they followed her, presuming that she was going to the tomb to weep there. When Mary came to where Jesus was and saw him, she fell at his feet and said to him, "Lord, if you had been here, my brother would not have died." When Jesus saw her weeping and the Jews who had come with her weeping, he became perturbed and deeply troubled, and said, "where have you laid him?" They said to him, "Sir, come and see." And Jesus wept. So the Jews said, "See how he loved him." But some on them said, "Could not the one who opened the eyes of the blind man have done something so that this man would not have died?"

So Jesus, perturbed again, came to the tomb. It was a cave, and a stone lay across it. Jesus said, Take away the stone." Martha, the dead man's sister said to him, "Lord, by now there will be a stench; he has been dead for four days." Jesus said to her, "Did I not tell you that if you believe you will see the glory of God?" So they took away the stone. And Jesus raised his eyes and said, "Father, I thank you for hearing me. I know that you also hear me; but because of the crowd here I have said this, that they may believe that you sent me." And when he had said this, he cried out in a load voice, "Lazarus come out!" The dead man came out, tied hand and foot with burial bands, and his face was wrapped in a cloth. So Jesus said to them, "Untie him and let him go." John 11:1-44

Now in Joppa there was a disciple named Tabitha (which translated means Dorcas). She was completely occupied with good deeds and almsgiving. Now during those days she fell sick and died, so after washing her, they laid [her] in a room upstairs. Since Lydda was near Joppa, the disciples, hearing that Peter was there, sent two men to him with the request, "Please come to us without delay." So Peter got up and went with them. When he arrived, they took him to the room upstairs where all the widows came to him weeping and showing him the tunics and cloaks that Dorcas had made while she was with them. Peter sent them all out and knelt down and prayed. Then he turned to her body and said, "Tabitha, rise up." She opened her eyes ,saw Peter, and sat up. He gave her his hand and raised her up, and when he had called the holy ones and the widows, he presented her alive. This became known all over Joppa, and many came to believe in the Lord. And he stayed a long time in Joppa with Simon, a tanner. Acts 9:36-43

It is common human experience that people who die do not come back to life yet there are examples in the bible where the dead do come back to life. In the old testament Elisha raises the Shunammite's son and brings him back to life. Jesus raises the man from Naim, Jairus's daughter and Lazarus. People who had died were brought back to life. In the book of Acts, Peter restores Tabitha to life. All of these were miracles performed by God through the intervention of man and the Son of Man.

# GIVING SIGHT TO THE BLIND

And as Jesus passed on from there, two blind men followed [him], crying out, "Son of David, have pity on us!" When he entered the house, the blind men approached him and Jesus said to them, "Do you believe that I can do this?" "Yes Lord", they said to him. Then he touched their eyes and said, "Let it be done for you according to your faith." And their eyes were opened. Jesus warned them sternly, "See that no one knows about this." But they went out and spread word of him through all that Land. Matthew 9: 27-31

As they left Jericho, a great crowd followed him. Two blind men were sitting by the roadside, and when they heard, that Jesus was passing by, they cried out, "[Lord,] son of David have pity on us!" The crowd warned them to be silent, but they called out all the more, "Lord, son of David, have pity on us!" Jesus stopped and called them and said, "What do you want me to do for you?" They answered him, "Lord, let our eyes be opened." Moved with pity, Jesus touched their eyes. Immediately they received their sight, and followed him. Matthew 20:29-34

The blind and the lame approached him in the temple area, and he cured them. Matthew 21:14

When they arrived at Bethsaida, they brought to him a blind man and begged him to touch him. He took the blind man by the hand and led him outside the village. Putting spittle on his eyes he laid his hands on him and asked, "Do you see anything?" Looking up he replied, "I see people looking like trees and walking." Then he laid hands on his eyes a second time and he saw clearly; his sight was restored and he could see everything distinctly. Then he sent him home and said, "Do not even go into the village." Mark 8:22-26

They came to Jericho. And as he was leaving Jericho with his disciples and a sizable crowd, Bartimaeus, a blind man , the son of Timaeus, sat by the roadside begging. On hearing that it was Jesus of Nazareth, he began to cry out and say, "Jesus, son of David, have pity on me." And many rebuked him, telling him to be silent. But he kept calling out all the more, "Son of David, have pity on me." Jesus stopped and said, "Call him." So they called the blind man, saying to him, "Take courage; get up, he is calling you." He threw aside his cloak, sprang up, and came to Jesus. Jesus said to him in reply, "What do you want me to do for you?" The blind man replied to him , "Master, I want to see." Jesus told him , "Go your way; your faith has saved you." Immediately he received his sight and followed him on the way. Mark 10: 46-52

Now as he approached Jericho a blind man was sitting by the roadside begging, and hearing a crowd going by, he inquired what was happening. They told him, "Jesus of Nazareth is passing by." He shouted, "Jesus, son of David, have pity on me!" The people walking in front rebuked him, telling him to be silent, but he kept calling out all the more, "son of David have pity on me!" Then Jesus stopped and ordered that he be brought to him; and when he came near, Jesus asked him, "What do you want me to do for you?" He replied, "Lord, please let me see." Jesus told him , "Have sight; your faith has saved you." He immediately received his sight and followed him, giving glory to God. When they saw this, all the people gave praise to God. Luke 18:35-43

As he passed by he saw a man blind from birth. His disciples asked him, Rabbi, who sinned, this man or his parents, that he was born blind?" Jesus answered, " Neither he nor his parents sinned; it is so that the works of God might be made visible through him. We have to do the works of the one who sent me while it is day. Night is coming when no one can work. While I am in the world I am the light of the world." When he had said this, he spat on the ground and made clay with the saliva, and smeared the clay on his eyes, and said to him, "Go wash in the Pool of Siloam" (which means sent). So he went and washed, and came back able to see.

His neighbors and those who had seen him earlier as a beggar said, "Isn't this the one who used to sit and beg?" Some said, "It is," but others said, "No, he just looks like him." He said, "I am". So they said to him, [So] how were your eyes opened?" He replied, "The man called Jesus made clay and anointed my eyes and told me , 'Go to Siloam and wash.' So I went there and washed and was able to see." And they said to him, "where is he?" He said, " I don't know."

They brought the one who was once blind to the Pharisees. Now Jesus had made clay and opened his eyes on a sabbath. So then the Pharisees also asked his how he able to see.; He said to them, he put clay on my eyes, and I washed, and now I can see." So some of the Pharisees said, "This man is not from God, because he does not keep the sabbath." [But] others said , "How can a sinful man do such signs?" And there was a division among them. So they said to the blind man again, "What do you have to say about him since he opened your eyes?" He said, "He is a prophet."

Now the Jews did not believe that he had been blind and gained his sight until they summoned the parents of the one who had gained his sight. They asked them, "Is this your son , who you say was born blind? How does he now see?" His parents answered and said, "We know that this is our son and that he was born blind. We do not know how he sees now, nor do we know who opened his eyes. Ask him, he is of age; he can speak for himself." His parents said this because they were afraid of the Jews, for the Jews had already agreed that if anyone acknowledged him as the Messiah, he would be expelled from the synagogue. For this reason his parents said, "He is of age; question him…"

So a second time they called the man who had been blind and said to him, "Give God the praise! We know that this man is a sinner." He replied, "If he is a sinner, I do not know. One thing I do know is that I was blind and now I see." So they said to hmi, "what did he do to you? How did he open your eyes?" He answered them, "I told you already and you did not listen. Why do you want to hear it again? Do you want to become his disciples, too?" They ridiculed him and said, "You are that man's disciple; we are disciples of Moses, but we do not know where this one is from." The man answered and said to them , "This is what is so amazing, that you do not know where he is from, yet he opened my eyes. We know that God does not listen to sinners, but if one is devout and does his will, he listens to him. It is unheard of that anyone opened the eyes of a person born blind. If this man were not from God, he would not be able to do anything." They answered and said to him, "You were born totally in sin, and you are trying to teach us ?" Then they threw him out.

When Jesus heard that they had thrown him out, he found him and said, "Do you believe in the Son of Man?" He answered and said, "Who is he, sir, that I may believe in him?" Jesus said to him, "you have seen him and the one speaking with you is he." He said, "I do believe, Lord." And he worshipped him. Then Jesus said, "I came into the world for judgement, so that those who do not see might see, and those who do might become blind."

Some of the Pharisees who were with him heard this and said to him , "Surely we are not also blind, are we?" Jesus said to them, "If you were blind you would have no sin; but now you are saying, 'We see,' so your son remains. John 9:1-41

Even the best ophthalmologists can rarely restore sight to the blind and not even these can restore the sight of one born blind. Jesus by touch or word does restore the sight of the blind on multiple occasions. These are miracles and demonstrate he was the son of God.

# HEALING THE LEPERS

Naaman, the army commander of the king of Aram, was highly esteemed and respected by his master, for through him the LORD had brought victory to Aram. But valiant as he was, the man was a leper. Now the Arameans had captured from the land of Israel in a raid a little girl, who became the servant of Naaman's wife. She said to her mistress, "If only my master would present himself to the prophet in Samaria! He would cure him or his leprosy."

Naaman went and told his master, "This is what the girl from the land if Israel said." The king of Aram said, "Go, I will send along a letter to the king of Israel." So Naaman set out, taking along ten silver talents, six thousand gold pieces, and ten festal garments.

He brought the king of Israel the letter, which read: "With this letter I am sending my servant Naaman to you, that you may cure of him of his leprosy." When he read the letter, the king of Israel tore his garments and exclaimed: "Am I a God with power over life and death, that this man should send someone for me to cuer him of leprosy? Take note! You can see he is only looking for a quarrel with me!" When Elisha, the man of God, heard that the king of Israel had torn his garments, he sent word to the king: "Why have you torn your garments? Let him come to me and find out there is a prophet in Israel."

Naaman came with his horses and chariots and stopped at the door of Elisha's house. Elisha sent him the message: "Go and wash seven times in the Jordan, and your flesh will heal, and you will be clean." But Naaman went away angry, saying, "I thought that he would surely come out to me and stand there to call on the name of the LORD his God, and would move his hand over the place, and thus cure the leprous spot. Are not the rivers of Damascus, the Abana and the Pharpar, better than the waters of Israel? Could I not wash in them and be cleansed? With this, he turned about in anger and left.

But his servants came up and reasoned with him: "My father, if the prophet told you to do something extraordinary, would you not do it? All the more since he told you, 'Wash, and be clean'?" So Naaman went down and plunged into the Jordan seven times, according to the word of the man of God. His flesh became again like the flesh of a little child, and he was clean. 2Kings5:1-14

When Jesus came down from the mountain, great crowds followed him. And then a leper approached, did him homage, and said, " Lord, if you wish, you can make me clean." He stretched out his hand, touched him, and said, "I will do it. Be made clean." His leprosy was cleansed immediately. Then Jesus said to him, "See that you tell no one, but go show yourself to the priest, and offer the gift that Moses prescribed; that will be proof for them." Matthew 8:1-4

A leper came to him [and kneeling down]] begged him and said, "If you wish, you can make me clean." Moved with pity, he stretched out his hand, touched him, and said to him, "I do will it. Be made clean." The leprosy left him immediately, and he was made clean. Then warning him sternly, he dismissed him at once. Then he said to him, "See that you tell no one anything, but go, show yourself to the priest and offer for your cleansing what Moses prescribed; that will be proof for them." The man went away and began to publicize the whole matter. He spread the report abroad so that it was impossible for Jesus to enter a town openly. He remained outside in deserted places, and people kept coming to him from everywhere. Mark 1:40-45

Now there was a man full of leprosy in one of the towns where he was; and when he saw Jesus, he fell prostate, pleaded with him, and said, "Lord, if you wish, you can make me clean." Jesus stretched out his hand, touched him, and said, "I do will it. Be made clean." And the leprosy left him immediately. Then he ordered him not to tell anyone, but "Go, show yourself to the priest and offer for your cleansing what Moses prescribed; that will be proof for them." The report about him spread all the more, and great crowds assembled to listen to him and to be cured of their ailments, but he would withdraw to deserted places to pray. Luke 5:12-16

As he continued his journey to Jerusalem, he traveled through Samaria and Galilee. As he was entering a village, ten lepers met [him]. They stood at a distance from him and raised their voice, saying, "Jesus, Mater! Have pity on us!" And when he saw them, he said,, "Go show yourselves to the priests." As they were going they were cleansed. And one of them, realizing he had been healed, returned, glorifying God in a loud voice; and fell at the feet of Jesus and thanked him. He was a Samaritan. Jesus said in reply, "Ten were cleansed, were they not? Where are the other nine? Has none but this foreigner returned to give thanks to God?" Then he said to him, "Stand up and go; your faith has saved you." Luke 17:11-19

Leprosy is a contagious disease that was found even in antiquity. IN biblical times leprosy was not curable and these people were avoided and ostracized. Jesus cures lepers with touch and word, truly a miracle.

# HEALING EVERY ILLNESS

He went around all of Galilee, teaching in their synagogues, proclaiming the gospel of the kingdom, and curing every disease and illness among the people. His fame spread to all of Syria, and they brought to him all who were sick with various diseases and racked with pain, those who were possessed, lunatics and paralytics, and he cured them. Matthew 4:23-24

When it was evening they brought him many who were possessed by demons, and he drove out the spirits by a word and cured all the sick, to fulfill what had been said by Isaiah the prophet: "He took away our infirmities and bore our diseases." Matthew 8:16-17

Jesus went around to all the towns and villages, teaching in their synagogues, proclaiming the gospel of the kingdom, and curing every disease and illness. Matthew 9:35

When Jesus realized this, he withdrew from that place. Many [people] followed him, and he cured them all. Matthew 12:15

After making the crossing, they came to land at Gennesaret. When the men of that place recognized him, they sent word to all the surrounding country. People brought to him all those who were sick and begged him that they might touch only the tassel on his cloak, and as many as touched it were healed. Matthew 14:34-36

Moving on from there Jesus walked by the sea of Galilee, went up on the mountain, and sat down there. Great crowds came to him, having with them the lame, the blind, the deformed, the mute, and many others. They placed him at his feet, and he cured them. The crowds were amazed when they saw the mute speaking, the deformed made whole, the lame walking, and the blind able to see, and they glorified the God of Israel. Matthew 15:29-31

When it was evening, after sunset, the brought to him all who were ill or possessed by demons. The whole town was gathered at the door. He cured many who were sick with various diseases, and he drove out many demons, not permitting them to speak because they knew him. Mark 1:32-34

He told his disciples to have a boat ready for him because of the crowd, so that they would not crush him. He had cured many and, as a result, those who had diseases were pressing upon him to touch him. Mark 3:9-10

He departed from there and came to his native place, accompanied by his disciples. When the sabbath came he began to teach in the synagogue, and many who heard him were astonished. They said, "Where did this man get all this? What kind of wisdom has been given him? What mighty deed Joses and Judas and Simon?" And they took offense at him. Jesus said to them, "A prophet is not without honor except in his native place and among his own kin and in his own house." So he was not able to perform any mighty deed there, apart from curing a few sick people by laying hands on them. He was amazed at their lack of faith. Mark 6:1-6

After making the crossing, they came to land at Gennesaret and tied up there. As they were leaving the boat, people immediately recognized him. They scurried about the surrounding country and began to bring in the sick on mats to wherever they heard he was. Whatever villages or towns or countryside he entered, they laid the sick in the marketplaces and begged him that they might touch only the tassel on his cloak; and as many who touched it were healed. Mark 6:53-56

At sunset, all who had people sick with various diseases brought them to him. He laid his hands on each of them and cured them. Luke 4:40

And he came down with them and stood on a stretch of level ground. A great crowd of the disciples and a large number of the people from ass Judea and Jerusalem and the coastal region of Tyre and Sidon came to hear him and to be healed of their diseases; and those who were tormented by unclean spirits were cured. Everyone in the crowd sought to touch him because power came forth from him and healed them all. Luke 6:17-19

He summoned the Twelve an gave them power and authority over all demons and to cure diseases, and he sent them to proclaim the kingdom of God and to heal [the sick]. Luke 9:1-22

*Some of God's Miracles*

Jesus healed everyone who came to him. Everyone! This is a miracle. Renal disease, heart disease, lung disease, cancer, autoimmune diseases- all diseases he cured. No physician before or after Jesus could accomplish the feat of healing thousands of all diseases. He was truly the divine physician. Touching Jesus or even the tassel of his cloak could cure them. By his very word people were cured of the illnesses. For those whose disease was caused by the persons sins Jesus even forgave their sin. This no modern day doctor can do. Jesus even cured some diseases that were uncurable like paralysis and blindness from birth. Jesus conferred his ability to cure disease on his apostles who performed the same healings as Jesus. Jesus's miraculous healings truly showed him to be the son of God for only God can perform the miracles that Jesus performed.

# HEALING THE CRIPPLED, THE LAME, AND THE PARALYTICS

When he entered Capernaum, a centurion approached him and appealed to him, saying, "Lord, my servant is lying at home paralyzed, suffering dreadfully." He said to him, "I will come and cure him." The centurion said in reply, "Lord, I am not worthy to have you enter under my roof; only say the word and my servant will be healed. For I too am a person subject to authority, with soldiers subject to me. And I say to one, 'Go,' and he goes; and to another, "Come here' and he comes; and to my slave, 'Do this' and he does it" When Jesus heard this he was amazed and said to those following him, "Amen, I say to you, in no one in Israel have I found such faith. I say to you, many will come from the east and the west, and will recline with Abraham, Isaac, and

Jacob at the banquet in the kingdom of heaven, but the children of the kingdom will be driven out into the outer darkness, where there will be wailing and grinding of teeth." And Jesus said to the centurion, "You may go; as you have believed, let it be done for you." And at that very hour [servant was healed]. Matthew 8:5-13

He entered a boat, made the crossing, and came into his own town. And these people brought to him a paralytic lying on a stretcher. When Jesus saw their faith, he said to the paralytic, "Courage child, your sins are forgiven." At that point some of the scribes said to themselves, "This man is blaspheming." Jesus knew what they were thinking, and said, "why do you harbor evil thoughts? Which is easier, to say 'Your sins are forgiven,' or to say, 'Rise and walk'? But that you may know that the Son of Man has authority on earth to forgive sins"—he then said to the paralytic, "Rise, pick up your stretcher, and go home.'" He rose and went home. When the crowds saw this they were struck with awe and glorified God who had given such authority to human beings. Matthew 9:1-8

When Jesus returned to Capernaum after some days, it became known that he was at home. Many gathered together so that there was no longer room for them, not even around the door, and he preached the word to them. They came bringing to him a paralytic carried by four men. Unable to get near Jesus because of the crowd, they opened up the roof above him. After they had broken through, they let down the mat on which the paralytic was lying. When Jesus saw their faith, he said to the paralytic, "Child your sins are forgiven." Now some of the scribes were sitting there asking themselves, "Why does this man speak that way? He is blaspheming. Who but God alone can forgive sins?" Jesus immediately in his mind what they were thinking to themselves, so he said, "Why are you thinking such things in your hearts? Which is easier, to save to the paralytic, 'Your sins are forgiven,' or to say, "Rise, pick up your mat and walk'? But that you may know that the Son of Man has authority to forgive sins on earth"—he said to the paralytic, "I say to you, rise pick up your mat and go home." He rose, picked up his mat at once, and went away in the sight of everyone. They were all astounded and glorified God, saying, "We have never seen anything like this." Mark 2:1-12

One day as Jesus was teaching, Pharisees and teachers of the law were sitting there who had come from every village of Galilee and Judea and Jerusalem, and the power of the Lord was with him for healing. And some men brought on a stretcher a man who was paralyzed; they were trying to bring him in and set [him] in his presence. But not finding a way to bring him in because of the crowd, they went up on the roof and lowered him on the stretcher through the tiles into the middle in front of Jesus. When he saw their faith, he said, "As for you, your sins are forgiven." Then the scribes and Pharisees began to ask themselves, "Who is this who speaks blasphemies? Who but God alone can forgive sins?" Jesus knew their thoughts and said to them in reply, "What are you thinking in your hearts? Which is easier, to say, 'Your sins are forgiven,' or to say, 'Rise and walk'? But that you may know that the Son of Man has authority on earth to forgive sins"—he said to the man who was paralyzed, "I say to you, rise pick up your stretcher and go home." He stood up immediately before them, picked up what he had been lying on, and went home, glorifying God. Then astonishment seized them all and they glorified God, and struck with are, they said, "We have seen incredible things today." Luke 5:17-26

He was teaching in a synagogue on the sabbath. And a woman was there who for eighteen years had been crippled by a spirit; she was bent over, completely incapable of standing erect. When Jesus saw her, he called to her and said, "Woman, you are set free of your infirmity." He laid his hands on her, and she at once stood up straight and glorified God. But the leader of the synagogue, indignant that Jesus had cured on the Sabbath, said to the crowd in reply, "There are six days when work should be done. Come on those days and be cured, not on the sabbath day." The Lord said to him in reply, "Hypocrites! Does not each of you on the sabbath untie his ox or his ass from the manger and lead it out for watering? This daughter of Abraham, whom Satan has bound for eighteen years now, ought she not have been set free on the sabbath day from this bondage?" When he said this, all his adversaries were humiliated; and the whole crowd rejoiced at all the splendid things done by him. Luke 13:10-17

Now Peter and John were going up to the temple area for the three o'clock hour of prayer. And a man crippled from birth was carried and placed at the gate of the temple called "the Beautiful Gate" every day to beg for alms from the people who entered the temple. When he saw Peter and John about to go into the temple, he asked for alms. But Peter looked intently at him, as did John, and said, "Look at us." He paid attention to them, expecting to receive something from them. Peter said, "I have neither silver nor gold, but what I do have I give you: in the name of Jesus Christ the Nazorean, [rise and ] walk." Then

Peter took him by the right hand and raised him up, and immediately his feet and ankles grew strong. He leaped up, stood, and walked around, and went into the temple with them, walking and jumping and Praising God, they recognized him as the one who used to sit begging at the Beautiful Gate of the temple, and they were filled with amazement and astonishment at what had happened to him. Acts 3:1-10

As Peter was passing through every region, he went down to the holy ones living in Lydda. There he found a man named Aeneas, who had been confined to bed for eight years, for he was paralyzed. Peter said to him, "Aeneas, Jesus Christ heals you. Get up and make your bed." He got up at once. And all the inhabitants of Lydda and Sharon saw him, and they turned to the Lord. Acts 9:32-35

Paralysis in people is usually permanent and can be caused by a variety of diseases. Jesus repeatedly heals paralytics and restores them to full health. Other than miracles, this could not be accomplished.

# OTHER HEALTH MIRACLES

Jesus entered the house of Peter, and saw his mother-in-law lying in bed with a fever. He touched her hand, the fever left her, and she rose and waited on him. Matthew 8:14-15

On leaving the synagogue he entered the house of Simon and Andrew with James and John. Simon's mother-in-law lay sick with a fever. They immediately told him about her. He approached, grasped her hand, and helped her up. The fever left her and she waited on them. Mark 1:29-31

After he left the synagogue, he entered the house of Simon. Simon's mother-in-law was afflicted with a sever fever, and they interceded with him about her. He stood over her, rebuked the fever, and it left her. She got up immediately and waited on them. Luke 4:38-39

On a sabbath he went to dine at the home of one of the leading Pharisees, and the people there were observing him carefully. In front of him was a man suffering from dropsy. Jesus spoke to the scholars of the law in reply, asking, "Is it lawful to cure on the sabbath or not?" But they kept silent; so he took the man and, after he had healed him, dismissed him. Then he said to them, "Who among you, if your son or ox falls into a cistern would not immediately pull him out on the sabbath day?" But they were unable to answer his question. Luke 14:1-6

As they were going out, a demoniac who could not speak was brought to him, and when the demon was driven out the mute person spoke. The crowds were amazed and said, "Nothing like this has ever been seen in Israel." But eh Pharisees said, " He drives our demons by the prince of demons." Matthew 9:32-34

Moving on from there, he went into their synagogue. And behold, there was a man there who had a withered hand. They questioned him, "Is it lawful to cure on the sabbath?" so that they might accuse him. He said to them, "Which one of you who has a sheep that falls into a pit on the sabbath will not take hold of it and lift it out? How much more valuable a person is than a sheep. So it is lawful to do good on the sabbath." Then he said to the man, "Stretch out your hand." He stretched it out, and it was restored as sound as the other. But the Pharisees went out and took counsel against him to put him to death. Matthew 12:9-14

Again he entered the synagogue. There was a man there who had a withered hand. They watched him closely to see if he would cure him on the sabbath so that they might accuse him. He said to the man with the withered hand, "Come up here before us." Then he said to them, "Is it lawful to do good on the sabbath rather than to do evil, to save life rather than to destroy it?" But they remained silent. Looking around at them with anger and grieved at their hardness of heart, he said to the man, "Stretch out your hand." He stretched it out and his hand was restored. The Pharisees went out and immediately took counsel with the Herodians against him to put him to death. Mark 3:1-6

While he was still speaking, a crowd approached and in front was one of the Twelve, a man named Judas. He went up to Jesus to kiss him. Jesus said to him, "Judas, are you betraying the Son of Man with a kiss?" His disciples realized what was about to happen, and they asked, "Lord, shall we strike with a sword?" And one of them struck the high priests servant and cut off his right ear. But Jesus said in reply, "Stop, no more of this!" Then he touched the servant's ear and healed him. Luke 22:47-51

Again he left the district of Tyre and went by way of Sidon to the Sea of Galilee, into the district of the Decapolis. And people brought to him a deaf man who had a speech impediment and begged him to lay his hand on him. He took him off by himself away from the crowd. He put his finger into the man's ears, and spitting, touched his tongue;; then he looked up to heaven and groaned, and said to him, *Ephphatha!* (that is, "Be opened!") And [ immediately] the man's ears were opened, his speech impediment was removed, and he spoke plainly. He ordered them not to tell anyone. But the more he ordered them not to,, the more they proclaimed it. They were exceedingly astonished and they said, "He has done all things well. He makes the deaf hear and [the] mute speak. Mark 7:31-37

Jesus performs miracles but treating people with fevers, who are deaf, who are mute, who suffer dropsy, who suffer from withered limbs, and who have had there ear severed. Clearly he was the son of God.

www.ingramcontent.com/pod-product-compliance
Lightning Source LLC
LaVergne TN
LVHW020423080526
838202LV00055B/5012